The Pug
with a Mug

Pam Scheunemann

Consulting Editor, Diane Craig, M.A./Reading Specialist

ABDO
Publishing Company

Published by ABDO Publishing Company, 4940 Viking Drive, Edina, Minnesota 55435.

Printed in the United States.

Credits
Edited by: Pam Price
Curriculum Coordinator: Nancy Tuminelly
Cover and Interior Design and Production: Mighty Media
Photo Credits: AbleStock, Brand X Pictures, Corbis Images, Digital Vision, Tracy Kompelien, Photodisc

Library of Congress Cataloging-in-Publication Data

Scheunemann, Pam, 1955-
    The pug with a mug / Pam Scheunemann.
        p. cm. -- (First rhymes)
    Includes index.
    ISBN 1-59679-513-1 (hardcover)
    ISBN 1-59679-514-X (paperback)
        1. English language--Rhyme--Juvenile literature. I. Title. II. Series.

PE1517.S4445 2005
808.1--dc22

                                                                              2005048037

SandCastle™ books are created by a professional team of educators, reading specialists, and content developers around five essential components that include phonemic awareness, phonics, vocabulary, text comprehension, and fluency. All books are written, reviewed, and leveled for guided reading and early intervention reading, and designed for use in shared, guided, and independent reading and writing activities to support a balanced approach to literacy instruction.

Let Us Know

After reading the book, SandCastle would like you to tell us your stories about reading. What is your favorite page? Was there something hard that you needed help with? Share the ups and downs of learning to read. We want to hear from you! To get posted on the ABDO Publishing Company Web site, send us e-mail at:

sandcastle@abdopub.com

SandCastle Level: Beginning

-ug

bug

jug

mug

pug

rug

This is a .

See the .

This is a .

He is a .

This is a .

The bug has wings.

The jug is brown.

The mug is black.

The pug is cute.

The rug is red.

The Pug
with a Mug

Here is a red rug.

On the red rug
sits a little pug.

The pug
on the red rug
has a big jug.

The pug
on the red rug
has a big jug
and a little mug.

A little bug
flies into the mug
by the pug
with the jug
on the rug!

About SandCastle™

A professional team of educators, reading specialists, and content developers created the SandCastle™ series to support young readers as they develop reading skills and strategies and increase their general knowledge. The SandCastle™ series has four levels that correspond to early literacy development in young children. The levels are provided to help teachers and parents select the appropriate books for young readers.

Emerging Readers
(no flags)

Beginning Readers
(1 flag)

Transitional Readers
(2 flags)

Fluent Readers
(3 flags)

These levels are meant only as a guide. All levels are subject to change.

To see a complete list of SandCastle™ books and other nonfiction titles from ABDO Publishing Company, visit **www.abdopub.com** or contact us at:
4940 Viking Drive, Edina, Minnesota 55435 • 1-800-800-1312 • fax: 1-952-831-1632